BUSINESS EMAILS DEMYSTIFIED

How to Upgrade Your Business Emails

Juliette Sander

Grosvenor House
Publishing Limited

This book is published by
Grosvenor House Publishing Ltd
Link House
140 The Broadway, Tolworth, Surrey, KT6 7HT.
www.grosvenorhousepublishing.co.uk

A CIP record for this book
is available from the British Library

ISBN 978-1-80381-426-1
eBook ISBN 978-1-80381-427-8

Disclaimer

Before we start our journey towards upgraded business emails, it is important to review a key disclaimer:

Data Protection and Other Regulations

Emailing people you do not have a personal or professional connection with can, in some cases, violate local laws and regulations. The European Union's General Data Protection Regulation (GDPR), for example, presents strict guidelines related to the collecting and processing of personal information. When emailing someone based in the EU, it is important that you research what the GDPR allows and doesn't allow you to do.

Several other countries around the world have similar regulations, so please check before reaching out to people located in different regions of the world.

The author of this book assumes no responsibility or liability for any mishandling of data or erroneous contacting.

For my parents, Gérard and Marie-Odile,
and my brother, Antoine – my three
fiercest supporters

"Email has an ability many channels don't: creating valuable, personal touches – at scale."
David Newman

Table of Contents

TABLE OF CONTENTS

Foreword

There's a saying amongst company founders: hire people who are better than you. This is the understatement of the century for Juliette.

When she started at Vorsight, there was a buzz about her ability to get meetings over email. She was A/B testing and measuring to know what worked. This caught my attention, so I investigated. Her cold email reply and conversion rates were higher than any we had ever seen. And we hired 453 SDRs over 16 years, so the sample size was not small.

We had a prodigy on our hands.

What do you do when you have a prodigy? Leverage her to make everyone else better of course!

We asked Juliette to teach her peer SDRs how to craft cold emails that booked first scheduled meetings. Soon enough all the SDRs were doubling or tripling their results from cold emails.

When Juliette told me she wrote Business Emails Demystified, it brought a big smile to my face.

How we teach kids to write in school has no connection to how they'll need to write business emails in their jobs. Juliette's book makes a huge difference in closing that gap.

There are two types of people: those who read a book like this then go back to their old ways and those who use what they learn to double their income.

Don't miss out on your opportunity to be the best business email writer in your company.

Steve Richard, co-founder, Vorsight & ExecVision

Introduction

Emails are at the center of everything we do. Whether personal or professional, we use emails every single day, multiple times a day. They are, in most professional environments, the most appropriate and most reliable way of contacting people. In fact, a 2012 McKinsey Global Institute analysis found that people spend 28% of their work week reading and answering emails[1] – if we convert that into hours, that's more than 10 hours in an average week, or over an entire day spent on emails!

Yet, most people have no idea what goes into writing a good email.

I have always been drawn to learning more about human cognition and how we interact with the world around us. For years, I studied Cognitive Science and Linguistics and learned more about our mind and intelligence than I could ever imagine. At its core, cognitive science is the study of the mind and everything that influences it, meaning that it is a mixture of psychology, computer science, philosophy, neuroscience, linguistics, sociology, and much more, each discipline exploring a different aspect of our psyche. Everything I learned was based on data and I ached for the real-life application of everything I was learning.

I spent the next few years putting pen to paper and collecting data on every single email I sent – both the good and the bad ones – to better understand where my knowledge of cognitive science and real-life experiences overlapped and embraced each other. More importantly, I wanted to record this intersection between disciplines so that others could replicate it.

When I first started my career as a Sales Development Representative, I was given a general 30-minute crash course on how to write emails – a course that is surprisingly often skipped in corporate onboarding. Most companies assume that hiring recent graduates means that they know how to write – which may well be true. But writing a successful email is very different from writing an essay, and is definitely a lot more complicated than writing a couple of words and pressing "send," hoping for the best. Emailing requires technique, timing, strategy, and an understanding of the human mind – which most people never learned.

I've held several sales roles over the years and each one required me to use my knowledge of cognitive science and human behavior to succeed. I observed my mentors and co-workers and over these past few years, I have come to realize that too many people don't know how to write emails that yield positive results.

The idea for this book stems from several email training and best practices sessions that I have led for a number of teams across different organizations. Realizing how big the knowledge gap is encouraged me to turn my knowledge into a book collecting the various psychology concepts and A/B tests that carried me through my career these past years.

This book gives you insights into foolproof business email strategies, maximizing positive results. This will completely overturn the way you view emails and, once practiced, you will never experience the writer's block we so often feel when staring at a blank email unsure where to start.

Now, if you've ever sent an email before, you'll know that there is no "one-shoe-fits-all" recipe. No one can tell you exactly what to write because this will vary depending on personas, goals, clients, time of the year, etc. What I can tell you, though, is that I have gathered here a collection of insights and trends, with data and psychology to back me up, which will drastically improve your email success. Some of the factors determining whether your email gets opened or answered don't depend on you, but most do – and those are the ones we will review.

This book is the combination of research, as well as working for and with over 50 clients spanning just as many industries. Over the course of these years, I have sent and analyzed over 350,000 emails.

My results, you ask?

- An average of 57.6% open rate, compared with a US national average of 21.5%[2]
- An average of 13.2% click rate, against a national average of 2.3%[3]
- An average of 15% email to meeting conversion rate
- Prospect meeting occurrence rate of 92% as a Sales Development Representative for a company with an average of 56%.

Keep in mind that although the advice in this book may also be relevant for emailing people you personally know, the content mostly revolves around emailing and establishing a connection with people you do not already have a relationship with.

That being said, this book is for anyone whose job includes heavy email writing. This book is for anyone who's ever had to write a professional email and had no idea where to start. This book is for anyone who feels out of touch with modern communication. This book is for anyone looking to strengthen their email writing skills.

I hope this book helps you kill the email game and work smarter, not harder.

Let's dive in!

CHAPTER ONE

Subject Lines

After making the switch from Account Manager to Customer Success Manager, I took a few days to better understand my new role and to apply everything I knew about emails. In all honesty, in those first few days, I decided to play it safe. I was very eager to make a great impression as a new hire and to ensure my team trusted me to reach out to users but, having transitioned to a new industry, I was worried that my instincts were off and that I might damage some existing relationships with clients.

So, my first emails were very safe, very clean, and not very inspiring. The content was fine, but the subject line was frankly boring, and as a new hire, I craved success. The email's purpose was to get inactive users – i.e. people who hadn't looked at our research in several months – back on the platform. The email was sent to a couple hundred people with the subject line "Access to [my company's name]."

Needless to say, the results weren't great.

13% open rate. Definitely not my best work.

Technically, this subject line said everything I needed it to say – my email was about access to my company's platform. But it wasn't exciting or intriguing.

The next morning, I decided to re-strategize and analyze what I had done. I had another couple hundred emails to send with the same idea and decided to change the subject line for something more daring. It became "You're missing out on [company's name] resources."

And BAM. A 70% open rate.

That was a 440% increase in open rate just with one basic, but major, change.

The subject line contains the first words a recipient sees when you send them an email. They set the tone for the entire correspondence and are a driving factor in whether someone opens your email.

Yet so many people neglect them, thus compromising their chances of their email getting opened and of creating a meaningful connection with their contacts.

To illustrate the importance of subject lines, SuperOffice, the European customer relationship management (CRM) software, ran a study and found that 33% of people open emails based on subject line alone.[4] Clearly, they are not to be taken lightly.

In this book, I cover emails from top to bottom and we therefore look at subject lines first. However, they should actually be the *last* part of the email you write. Before knowing exactly how you want to formulate your subject line, you should have your email's entire body fleshed out and ready to go before starting work on your subject line. Use everything you wrote in your email to carve the best one-liner possible.

In this chapter, we will go over some best practices, as well as the different types of subject lines.

Topic

Write a subject line that is not relevant, and you will be ignored every time. The executives you're reaching out to don't have time to read irrelevant emails – they barely have time to read the relevant ones. This means that yours needs to stand out by promising to tell them something important and useful to *them*.

In other words, your subject line should evoke some emotion in your reader, making them think that not reading your email would be worse than reading it. This is the first thing they will read, and you need to hook them in to get their curiosity and interest piqued.

Your first task when writing a subject line is to map out exactly which emotion you are trying to evoke in your reader.

After testing out an enormous number of subject lines myself and extensively researching the topic, here are the subject line type that tend to perform best:

Type	Explanation	Examples
FOMO (Fear Of Missing Out)	No one likes missing out on anything, and especially not the tool that could make them more efficient in their job and generate more revenue for their company. Create that feeling of missing out in your recipients	• You're missing out on [Company name] resources • Your team is registered – are you?
Referrals	Sometimes, you are emailing this specific person because someone else recommended them to you.	• Referred to you by John Smith • John Smith sent me your way

Type	Explanation	Examples
	Maybe their boss, their co-worker, their partner who picked up the phone when you called… Whoever that person is, their name absolutely should be included in the subject line. A mention of my boss in the subject line will get my attention 100% of the time	• Looping you into my conversation with John Smith • Via John Smith
Celebratory	Is there a celebratory reason you are reaching out to these people specifically? Did they do something that attracted your attention and made you want to connect with them? If so, mention that in the subject line. Get them excited about reading your email too! Make them feel special!	• You're a top user • Great news – you now have access to [name of tool]
Promotions	If you're planning on offering this person a free trial or a free gift, the subject line is a great place to introduce that – everyone loves free things and the idea that someone wants to give us something tends to pique our curiosity.	• Personalized trial for [company name] • Congratulations! • Claim your gift today!

Type	Explanation	Examples
	⚠ One trap to avoid: a subject line that sounds too good to be true tends to raise suspicions and your recipient might think your email is a scam. Re-read your subject line and ask yourself how you would feel seeing it in your inbox	
Start a Conversation	At the very core, most emails are meant to open the door to a conversation – whether online or offline, you are often looking for your recipient to do or say something that will create a connection and invite you to talk more about your product, services, etc. A great subject line is one that hints at that conversation	• Have you seen this? • Let's chat about this • Hate this?
Pain Point	Some of your recipients will be more responsive to loss aversion,[5] meaning that they will be more intrigued by an email about fixing their pain	• Are you struggling with hiring? • Is your CRM blocked?

Type	Explanation	Examples
	point than one promising a positive result. They will be willing to pay more for a product that makes their lives easier. If you truly understand your recipient's pain point and are able to include it in the subject line, you will significantly increase the chances of someone opening your email	• Unlock your inspiration
Humor	Depending on who you're contacting, humor may be a great way to get your recipient's attention. Many people respond very positively to humor and are more willing to open an email with a joking subject line than a neutral one	• Since we can't all win the lottery… • [Insert dad joke] • Swipe right on us • It's Friday; you're probably killing time anyways
Break-Up Emails	Every now and then, there will be someone you've spoken to and had a great conversation, or you feel like they're low-hanging fruit, they have the most relevant title – whatever it is, they feel like a good fit. Yet, no matter what you do, they keep ignoring you.	• Did I miss you? • Before I go • Maybe next time

Type	Explanation	Examples
	The break-up email is the last email you send before moving on. As Cialdini's research[6] shows, people will go out of their way to behave consistently with past behavior and make right on their promises, so reminding them of their commitment can often do the trick and bring them back to you	

Bottom line is you want them to open your email. And your subject line is a direct window into what the email is about. So don't make your subject line boring – that would imply your email is boring.

Make it interesting.

Make it relevant.

Make it worth opening.

Personalization

Now that I've got you thinking about how to make your subject line more thought-provoking, you might be thinking about how to make it more personal and make your recipient feel special. The last thing we want when emailing people is for them to think they are just another name on a long list of people you are emailing and that they are receiving the exact same message as hundreds of other people.

The simple answer to the question of personalization is yes: personalize your subject lines as often as possible. In fact, Experian Marketing Services, a data-centric marketing company, found that personalizing subject lines can result in a 29% increase in open rates and a 41% increase in click rate[7] – quite a significant increase!

And luckily, there are many ways to personalize a subject line, so you can experiment to find which one fits best with your email. You can insert the recipient's company name, their first name, an interesting fact about them... Anything that will make the subject line less generic and sound like you're addressing them directly.

Now, your recipient will see that you are emailing *them* specifically and feel called out, thus increasing their likelihood of opening your email.

sales engagement platforms like Salesloft, Outreach, Marketo, FrontSpin, and more allow you to personalize your emails en masse using filters, rather than having to edit each individual email. This can make this process incredibly easy and rewarding if you're emailing several people at once, so you no longer have an excuse not to personalize your subject lines.

Word Count

Now that you have your personalized, thought-provoking subject line, let's look at its length. Given that the subject line is the first part of the email your recipient will see, you want to include enough to pique their interest. However, you don't want to make it so long that they don't read the whole line, or worse, their computer or phone cuts off the subject line and they're unable to read everything. As a rule of thumb, the average computer inbox shows 60 characters, whereas a phone inbox will show 30. So, after writing your subject line, ask yourself if it is too long to be properly read or if, on the contrary, it is too short to pique their curiosity.

If you've written emails before, or gotten any type of training on subject lines, you'll probably have heard that the shorter you keep your subject line, the better. The truth is, shorter is better, but somewhere in the middle is the actual soft spot. Marketo, a marketing automation software company, conducted a study[8] a few years ago looking at how long your subject line should be to maximize your chances of your email being clicked.

Looking at over 2 million emails and their subject lines, they found that emails with four words showed the highest open rate, at just over 18%. However, emails with seven words showed the highest overall engagement, meaning open and click to open rates, or the percentage of recipients who clicked on a link after opening the email (10.8%). The below table summarizes their findings:

Number of Words in Subject Line	Open Rate	Click to Open
4 Words	18.26%	8%
5 Words	17.10%	7 90%
6 Words	15.30%	10.10%
7 Words	15.20%	10.80%
8 Words	12.20%	6.60%
9 Words	10.30%	10.60%
10 + Words	13.70%	7.90%

This Marketo research clearly demonstrates that 7 words is the ideal subject line length to increase click rates, based on the marketing emails they studied. But what happens when you want to increase your response rate rather than your click rate? A Salesloft study[9] looking solely at sales emails found that subject lines with 4 words performed significantly better than longer ones when looking at response rates specifically. This difference could be due to people responding to emails based on subject lines but clicking on links based on the links themselves. Regardless, keeping a subject line short is crucial to the success of your campaign and depending on your desired outcome, you will want to adjust subject line length.

As you will notice throughout this book, you will want to structure your email differently based on what you are trying to accomplish. Next time you are writing an email, critically review your subject line – are all words in it necessary? Are they all adding to the point you are making in your email? If not, cut them to remain succinct and straight to the point, increasing your chances of receiving a response or of your recipient clicking on your email.

Questions

Another common concern is whether questions should be posed in subject lines. After all, if the idea is to capture the recipient's attention and encourage them to open the email, a question seems like an ideal way to pique their interest.

The honest answer is that it depends on the purpose of your email: if you are writing to your recipient with the intention of getting an answer to a question, then absolutely. For example, you might want to know more about how they are handling a specific challenge or if they can help you with a specific project. In most cases, our first reaction when we are asked a question is to answer it – and the same goes for emails. Seeing a question in a subject line will encourage your recipient to open your email and to answer your question.

In fact, Yesware, a sales productivity platform, did a study[10] on this topic and found that, when cold emailing people, subject lines asking a question resulted in open rates 10% higher than those without questions: the open rate for all subject lines was 39.71%, while the open rate for subject lines that are questions was 48.39%.

That being said, like most parts of your email, you always want to make sure that your choices emphasize your point. Asking a question just to ask a question, unrelated to what you are trying to convey in your email, may end up hurting you. You want to show that you are credible and can be trusted, that you're worthy of your recipient's time. Starting off with an out-of-place question or a question you never address in your email, for example, would harm the conversation you are trying to start with your recipient.

Remember – your subject line should pique interest and introduce your email in the most credible and trustworthy way.

Wording

Wording is a critical part of your subject line: phrase an idea the wrong way, and you could lose your recipient in a fraction of a second. Especially when you only have about seven words to convince someone to read your email!

Words to include in subject lines

Based on my trials with various combinations of wording and research on the topic, here is a short collection of words that can increase the likelihood of your email being opened:

Action Verbs	Congratulations	Event	News	Video
Alert	Daily	Introducing	Special	Weekly
Bulletin	A specific date	Invitation	Update	You / Your

Words not to include in subject lines

Unfortunately, spam filters are hard to bypass. Depending on who you are emailing, their system security, how many emails you're sending out, etc., you may be sent to people's spam folders, and, in most cases, there is very little you can do to avoid that.

However, while most criteria for spam filters are out of your control, there's one specific criterion you can act on: in 2018, Yesware conducted a study[11] and found that subject lines containing certain words were more likely to be sent directly to spam filters if the sender was external to the company or not a regular correspondent:

$	Cash	Increase	Order now	Stop
% off	Cheap	Limited time offer	Remove	Test
Apply now	Free	Miracle	Satisfaction guaranteed	Urgent

According to them, using any of these words in your subject line will increase the likelihood you will be considered as spam. If these words are in your usual roster, start replacing them!

Subject Line Examples

Many factors contribute to the success of a subject line. With this data in your back pocket, your email open rate will skyrocket. Take a look at the subject line examples below to see these tips in action.

First Email

- Reconnecting this week
- Referred by [referral name]
- Your team is registered – why aren't you?
- You're missing out on [company name] resources
- [Company name] has access!
- Trending content @ [company name]
- You're a top user
- Great news – you now have access
- [First name], what do you think?

Break-up Email

- Have you been eaten by alligators or are you just swamped?
- Did I miss you?
- Before I go
- 12/1 deadline
- Last attempt
- Closing the loop
- Bad timing
- Final follow-up

HOT TIP #1:
Use www.SubjectLineGrader.com to see how your subject line compares with others. It looks at criteria such as sentiment, word count, character count, word case, and more to give you an idea of how good your subject line is.

HOT TIP #2:
Use www.aminstitute.com/headline for a second opinion analyzing specifically the emotions your subject line will trigger in your recipient.

CHAPTER TWO

Email Body

People have now opened your email – congratulations! They have shown the first mark of interest and you are on your way to success. Now is your time to draw them in with the best email they have ever read. One so good that they have no other option than to click on your links or to schedule a meeting with you.

This chapter will teach you everything you need to know about crafting the body of your email, from greetings to email signatures, and everything in between.

Greeting

The first thing you will most likely write is the greeting – the first thing that people will read. You may think this has little impact, but you'd be wrong. In reality, this is one of the most important details in your entire email because people will see it in the email preview. This tiny piece of information will set the tone and formality of your email.

> **HOT TIP:**
> Drop the Mr. and Mrs. and call your recipient by their first name. People are much more likely to respond, and you will sound more credible, confident, and approachable.

Before we dive into email greetings, though, let's look at the power there is in skipping the email greeting altogether.

If I look at my inbox right now, every single email in there starts the same: some variation of "hello Juliette." And I'm willing to bet everyone you are emailing sees the exact same thing – tons of emails that start with the same classic greeting. Now don't get me wrong, there is nothing wrong with starting your email with a classic greeting. However, if you want to stand out in an inbox, try starting with a sentence no one else will be using.

For example, if you were emailing someone named John about a job opening in his department, you might want to try starting your email with "Researching your company, I noticed you were hiring, John."

This first sentence will now stand out in John's inbox, otherwise filled with "hi John" equivalents. The sharpness of this first sentence may not be for everyone – but you'd be surprised how successful this technique is.

If you are looking for a way to differentiate yourself in someone's inbox, skipping the greeting is a great way to do so.

If you do want to use greetings, however, let's start by reviewing the most popular ones through the lens of your recipient to see what these greetings say about your email:

Phrase	How it Feels to the Recipient
To whom it may concern	You have no idea who you are writing to and really don't care to find out, or to sound nice. You care very little for their response and while you're trying very hard to be polite, you're coming across as very out of-touch with the business world
Greetings	You're very formal and perhaps a little uptight. You create distance between you and other people and lack sympathy and simplicity
Dear [first name]	Usually used to address people we respect and cherish. The word "dear" itself refers to someone or something close to our heart and anticipates a heartfelt note.

Phrase	How it Feels to the Recipient
	A professional email to someone you have never met and do not have a close relationship with is not the best place for this greeting
[First name]	You have something very formal and important to say to your recipient and don't even have time for hellos
Hi [first name]	Simple and straight to the point; you are direct and easy-going, ready to get down to business
Hello [first name]	Similar to "hi," you are very direct and go for simplicity, although you like to be more formal in your introduction
Hey [first name]	You are probably quite young and informal, getting rid of any distance between you and your recipient. You clearly write a lot of emails and seem approachable

So, now that we know what they say about you, which one should you use? Which message would be most successful in a business email?

We're not the only ones asking this question. In 2018, Brendan Greenley[12] conducted a study looking at over 300,000 different email threads. As we can see in the table below, they found that five greetings were used most often: "hey," "hello," "hi," "dear," and "greetings."

These five greetings, however, all yielded different response rates:

Greeting	Response Rate
"Hey"	64%
"Hello"	53.6%
"Hi"	62.7%
"Greetings"	57.2%
"Dear"	56.5%
All emails	47.5%

As you can see, out of all those greetings, one stood out as yielding the biggest number of responses: "hey."

According to Greenley, people were more likely to respond to an email that started with "hey" than one that started with "dear." As we saw, "hey" is the least formal greeting and the most inviting one.

If you're ever tempted to neglect your greeting again, remember this chapter and think again. Your greeting will be in the preview in your recipient's inbox, so make sure to choose one that encourages them to open your email.

Body

Now that you have the greeting, the next step is to write the body of your email. Definitely the longest and most time-consuming part of your email. I recommend that you split it into three parts or paragraphs:

- the reason
- the story
- the ask.

This model will allow you to hit all the major points you want to hit, in an organized way.

The Reason

Let's start with the reason you are reaching out to them, which should be your first paragraph. This is what gets your recipient hooked into what you are writing to them. To do this, you want to lay out very clearly why you are reaching out to them specifically. People get so many emails nowadays, many sent by bots, so how do you stand out?

The only way to encourage people to continue reading is if they feel like your email is relevant to *them*, so try to create some personal connection to make your recipient feel they are not just a name on a list (even if they are).

For example, you may be reaching out to them because there's a job opening in their department, or because they have the perfect title to make great use of the software you are selling. Regardless, you need them to feel targeted.

In this first paragraph, you want to center everything around them: an article they were recently quoted in, an interesting project they're working on, a cool experience you saw on their LinkedIn... there are thousands of different ways of doing this! Sometimes even just mentioning their title is enough to draw people in – anything that is about them works.

If you're not sure where to start, ask yourself: why am I writing to this person? Is it their title? Is it their experience? Is it that they went to the same college as me and I'm hoping they can help me get a referral to someone? Why are they of interest to me and why should they keep reading my email instead of deleting it or passing it to someone else?

For personalized emails, it will be very easy for you to integrate personal details in this first paragraph. When mass emailing, try to find a hook that everyone on your list has in common (their geography, their company, their team, a project they are working on). You may have to segment lists in different ways (more on this later) but adding some personalization in this first sentence will go a long way for you.

There are many different places to go when looking for information on a person or company. Usually called pre-call research (PCR), you can find this information in various places online:

- Internet search
- LinkedIn / Sales Navigator
- Company website
- Your CRM tool
- ZoomInfo, Seamless.AI, and other data platforms with business and employee information

The Story

Next, you want to introduce the purpose of your email – the story. This is where you connect their experience from your first paragraph to what your company does and how you can be of value.

This part will most likely take the longest to write because this is the real meat of your email – your moment to shine. When reading this paragraph, you want your recipient to feel involved in what you are explaining. And the best way to get them involved is by telling them a story.

Whether this takes the form of content links, a sales pitch, or a customer story, that is entirely up to you, but you want your recipient to understand how you ended up in their inbox today. And this should resonate with the person reading it.

Simon Sinek said it best in his 2009 Ted Talk[13] with his golden circle concept: "every single person, every single organization on the planet knows what they do, 100 percent. Some know how they do it... But very, very few people or organizations know why they do what they do."

That *why* is what will make the difference in every email, every deal, every job you ever work on. Why do you do what you do? Why does your company do what it does? And why does it matter?

Without being able to answer that question, it will be very difficult for you to show value in what you mention in your email – and therefore harder to get the outcome you want.

Let me give you an example to illustrate how much more important it is to know *why* your company exists than *how* it works:

The first company I worked for, Vorsight, was an outsourced sales company, meaning we were helping other companies build their sales pipeline. We were their Sales Development Representatives and worked to get meetings for them and create opportunities for new business.

When we first started working with a new client, we usually had a few hours to research the client and familiarize ourselves with the product, but we were expected to start emailing, calling, and scheduling meetings within a day or two. We didn't have time to learn about the ins and outs of the product or memorize fancy stats. We created our pitch from scratch with only the very basics of the company in mind.

And as it turns out, that's all we needed. As long as we understood *why* the company was created, we were golden.

When you craft your email, think about the *why* behind your product, service, company, resume: *why do you do what you do?*

However, while focusing on your *why*, it's important to remember that this part of your email should tell a story. Omit your confusing stats, promised ROI, and price listings. Focus on your *why* and forget about the numbers and buzzwords that make all our eyes roll. While they may all be true, and your results might be that impressive, keep those for a sales pitch or interview. For now, focus on getting your recipient's attention long enough to be intrigued by your purpose and the problem you fix or gap you bridge.

If you're unsure how to create this *why*, start by looking at your company's mission – every company has a blurb about how and why they were created, so use that as inspiration. If you are selling yourself rather than a company, think about your professional experience: why are you looking to sell yourself to this specific person?

Lastly, when writing this paragraph, think about how you can center your email around your recipient. Everything you write here should be about them and how you can benefit *them*. It does not matter that other clients love you. It does not matter that you have 10 years of experience in the field. What matters is how that *relates to your recipient and their work.*

When reading your email, they should understand how you can help respond to a need they have, or pain point they are experiencing. Help people visualize how you can help them find a solution to the problems that keep them up at night.

HOT TIP:
If you find that your emails contain a lot of "I," try flipping those to "you" and changing the narrative to center around your recipient instead of yourself.

Here are some questions to ask yourself to inspire your *why*:

- For cold outreach:

  o How was the company created? What was the idea behind it? What problem is it trying to solve?

  o What is your biggest success story?

  o How did you help your most successful client?

  o Who else in the industry is using your services or product?

- For warm leads:

  o What has changed since you last emailed this person? Why were updates made?

  o Why is now better timing than last time you connected?

The Ask

Now that you've made it this far into your email and have a great greeting, reason, and story, let's look at the next major part of your email – your call to action (CTA). Most emails will end with an action for the recipient to take – accept a meeting, engage on your website, show interest in a product, etc.

Most often, your call to action or, as I like to call it, your ask, will come at the end of your email, once you have introduced the purpose of your outreach. This is your chance to get your recipient to react to everything you introduced above.

However, before diving into CTAs, it's important to note that not all emails should have a CTA and they can sometimes be skipped. For example, if you write newsletters for a magazine, there is a chance your newsletters won't have a CTA. Their purpose is solely to introduce new content to your readers and there is no distinct action for them to take, other than read the information presented.

If you are writing an email with a CTA, though, they can be quite intimidating if you're not sure what to write. CTAs are your ending statement, your chance to summarize your point, and more importantly, your chance to make your ask. This is your moment, so make sure to seize it!

Before I go into the details of CTAs, let's take a look at the most common types:

Call To Action	Explanation
The Meeting Request	By far the most common and popular, this is exactly what it sounds like – asking your recipient for a meeting
Interest Gauge	Sometimes you're just here for a temperature check, or want a softer close to your first cold email, so you just gauge interest
Feedback Request	You want to know more about how your service, product, or company is perceived and are asking people directly for that feedback
Platform Engagement	A technique consisting of sending some links to content with the hope that people will click on them and read more information
Webinar / Event Registration	If you are hosting a webinar or an event (or for anything else that people need to register for) and advertising it, you will want people to register
Content Download	You are offering some free content that people can download straight from your email and you are encouraging them to take advantage of that
Free Trial	Inviting the recipient to a free trial of the product or service your company is selling

These are probably the most common CTAs, but of course there are others too. There are an infinite number and the most important aspect of your CTA is that you find the one that makes sense in your context and concludes your email in a relevant and useful way.

But before you get carried away with CTAs, one important note: your email should only have **one CTA**. People get distracted easily and asking too much of them at once will only result in losing them or getting partial answers. So, make sure you have one, clear, straightforward ask. Follow-up questions can come in a later email or conversation once you've gotten their initial commitment.

In general, CTAs are the reason you are reaching out to a person in the first place, so it should be clear to you which route you should go, and which type you should pick. However, the hard part is what comes next: how do you formulate this CTA in a compelling way, encouraging your reader to do whatever it is you want them to do?

RULE #1: use strong action words to encourage your reader to act. Make it very clear what you are asking for and use the appropriate language to convey the emotions you are looking for in your reader (urgency, curiosity, etc.).

RULE #2: no matter which type of CTA you choose, it will always come in two parts: the summary of the situation, and the actual ask itself. Whether you separate those into two sentences or combine them into one, or whether you start with the ask and end with the summary, does not really matter. All that matters is that both parts are present to increase clarity and nudge your recipient just enough for them to act.

So, let's look at this first part I mention: the summary of the situation. Since this will be your closing paragraph and the last chance to convince your recipient to agree to do whatever you are hoping they'll do, you want to make sure that they understand your argument.

Very often, people will skim your email until they get to the end, to see what your email is all about. People wait for you to summarize in the last paragraph so they can read only those couple of lines and then decide, based on those, whether the rest of the email is worth reading. So, these lines need to be compelling, using strong action verbs and making them feel like they would be missing out on something if they didn't do as you suggest.

For example, if I were summarizing an email in which I am looking to book a meeting with a marketing executive to talk about my marketing software, I might formulate it like this:

"Let's find some time to connect on what other companies are doing to create positive interactions with their brand."

Why did I formulate my sentence like this? Let's review:

- It makes it clear that I'm asking for a call
- Mentioning other companies creates a sense of missing out and piques their curiosity for competitor insights
- "Positive interactions with their brand" is what I identified as this executive's pain point: the topic that keeps them up at night.

Now that we have our summary statement, let's take a look at the second part of this CTA: the actual ask. Usually just one short sentence, this is your final opportunity to get a "yes."

All the examples I wrote above when talking about the different types of CTA are great examples of this: if asking for a call, this sentence can be as simple as asking for their availability. If asking them to click on links, then just say that. This will probably be the easiest part to write since it is all about writing down exactly what you hope they will do now that they have read your entire email (or at least got to the bottom of it).

Unfortunately, no matter how beautiful your CTA is, there are no guarantees your recipient will respond to you. However, there are a few ways to increase the likelihood. After all, writing an email is nothing if not an exercise in social psychology, and we all know that how we frame and phrase our asks influences how receptive people will be to them.

The meeting CTA seems often to be the most complicated one because you are asking for a higher level of commitment. The recipient is not just taking a few seconds out of their day to respond to you or click on a link, but they are committing to 20–30 minutes of their time to talk with you, so I'm going to spend a little time looking at the meeting request CTA.

One of the biggest questions is always: how do I offer time? Do I let the recipient suggest a time? Do I offer some available times?

In 2020, Gong Labs, the research entity of the call recording platform, ran a study on over 300,000 emails to find the best way to formulate your CTA.[14] The three CTAs they studied were:

- the "specific CTA," which offers a specific time and date for a meeting
- the "open-ended CTA," which does not offer a specific time or date but rather a timeframe ("are you available next week?")
- the "interest CTA," which does not ask for time but instead gauges the recipient's interest on the topic you wrote to them about ("would you be interested in learning more?").

What they found is that when cold emailing someone, the interest CTA performed significantly better than the two other CTAs:

- the "specific CTA" yielded a 15% success rate
- the "open-ended CTA" yielded a 13% success rate
- the "interest CTA" yielded a 30% success rate.

This means that next time you should try asking them about their interest and opening a conversation with them over email before jumping straight into asking for a meeting. As Gong Lab concludes in their study, "sell the conversation, not the meeting."

That being said, ChiliPiper, a meeting scheduling app, did dive deeper into how to ask for time, and here's what they found:

Out of 300 full-time business professionals included in their study, they found that 75% preferred booking meetings when times were suggested rather than picking a time themselves on someone's calendar.[15] When recipients are left to choose times by themselves, they are quickly confronted by information overload and are too overwhelmed by options to choose one. For many business professionals, the process of comparing their calendar to the hundreds of options on yours is too time-consuming and they quickly give up.

However, having three or four suggested times pre-selected for them makes it easier for them to browse through and pick their favorite in very little time.

So, next time you are asking someone for their time, try to suggest a couple of timeframes that work on your end and let them decide when is most convenient out of those options.

HOT TIP:
Link your calendar for all options to eliminate some back and forth and to facilitate meeting booking in one click.

Sign-Off

You may have realized by now that nothing in emails is a detail. Every single part of it will contribute to the open, click, and response rates, and ultimately will determine whether your recipient engages with you. Your sign-off is no exception. While they may not have the same obvious importance as subject lines and email content, sign-offs are a final opportunity to show your recipient respect and end your email on a high note.

The serial position effect,[16] more commonly known as the primacy and recency effect, confirms that even the end of your email matters. People remember most the beginning and the end of an event, and rarely the middle. In the original study, which has been replicated dozens of times since, participants were asked to memorize a list of 40 words. The results showed that the first and last words were remembered significantly more often than the words in the middle.

If you think about it, this makes sense – we pay attention in the beginning because we are trying to remember, then our focus shifts elsewhere, we get distracted and overwhelmed by the data, and in the end, we re-shift our focus to process the conclusion and will react based on what entered our brain most recently.

This concept is very popular among college students, who can save an entire paper with strong opening and closing paragraphs. This can also be applied to email writing. Your recipients will always remember most the beginning of your email and the very end.

Clearly the email sign-offs are important. So, how can we maximize their impact?

You've probably already gotten to the end of an email and wondered what to say. From "sincerely" to "warmly," and from "regards" to "kindly," it can be somewhat overwhelming to decide which is best to use. Personally, I'm in the very boring "best" category, and if you've worked in the business world long enough, you've probably heard many managers say that "best" is the most compelling sign-off there is.

But here's where things get interesting. As it turns out, "best" is not the sign-off that gets the most replies. In fact, using "best" may be negatively impacting your response rate.

A 2017 Boomerang study[17] analyzed over 350,000 emails ranging from support emails to university communications and their response rates, and found that the best sign-offs are in fact:

Sign-Off	Response Rate
Thanks in advance	67.5%
Thanks	63%
Thank you	57.9%
Best	51.2%

From this study, we can clearly see a pattern of gratitude: people are more likely to respond when the sign-off includes a thankful message. Feeling gratitude from someone motivates people to help and to act.

In fact, many studies show how important expressing gratitude is when encouraging someone to do something. In 2010, Adam M. Grant and Francesco Gino ran an experiment[18] where participants were asked to give feedback to "Eric," a job applicant. After sending their feedback, participants got a response from "Eric" asking them a second favor: feedback on a cover letter he wrote. In Eric's response, half of the participants were thanked for their initial feedback before being asked for more feedback, while the other half of the participants were only asked for more feedback, without being thanked for the original feedback.

Grant and Gino then observed how many participants in each group provided "Eric" with additional feedback. Turns out, 66% of people who were thanked for their

feedback agreed to help with the cover letter, versus 32% in the group that was not thanked for their feedback. A simple "thank you" increased the likelihood of receiving help by over 100%.

So if, like me, "best" has always been your go-to sign-off, you might want to rethink that one and become more thankful to your recipients. The results will speak for themselves.

Email Signature

Lastly, your email should always end with a professional signature. Most people will only ever look at your signature if they are wondering what your title is or if they are looking for your phone number. However, the email signature is similar to your attire on a job interview – no one will pay attention to it if it looks professional and good, but everyone will notice it if it looks sloppy. Your email signature is a sign that your business is legit and that you are a professional. Plus, emails are an extra way to market yourself and an opportunity to have your recipient notice your name and company, familiarizing them with your brand.

A few things you want to make sure to always include in your signature:

- **Your first and last name** – seems obvious, but, surprisingly, I have seen some people forget to include it
- **Your title** – the main point of interest people will be looking for in your signature so they can get a better idea of who emailed them, and why
- **Your company name and logo** – people need to know where you're writing from and including the logo makes it seem more legit. Some people are also more familiar with logos than names, especially if you're reaching out to international people, so including your company logo is crucial (think Nike or Apple)
- **Your company website** – similarly to the company name and logo, including the website adds legitimacy. It will also encourage people to check out your website for more information if they are interested
- **You phone number** – either personal or professional depending on your work and where you prefer people to call you
- [optional] **Your LinkedIn** – only include your LinkedIn link if your page looks clean and up to date. This is a great way to gain credibility by showing your resume and showcasing your brand
- [optional] **A calendar link** – makes it easier for people to book meetings with you in a few clicks of a button

- [optional] **Your pronouns** – becoming more and more common in email signatures, it's a great practice to make sure you are properly referred to and normalize adding pronouns in signatures, regardless of how you identify.

Tying It All Together

Your email is now written and nearly ready to be sent off! But before you do, check out the tips on language in chapter 5. And remember to re-read your entire email one last time, out loud.

A common tip when you are writing, proofreading out loud actually improves your ability to detect syntax errors, grammatical errors, and typos, as demonstrated in a 2022 study by Cushing and Bodner[19]. Reading your own emails aloud will allow you to catch any inconsistencies, as well as put you in your recipient's shoes, experiencing what it might be like for them to receive your email.

When proofreading your emails, make sure to pay attention to syntax, grammar, and typos, of course, but also pay attention to the overall flow – does your email sound too complex? Does it draw you in? Are you interested in responding to it? All these questions will help you determine whether your email is ready for send-off or needs another round of revisions.

Another proofreading tip is to have someone external to your project read your email. Very often, we write emails from our perspective, thinking that the recipient will understand what we are asking. However, remember that you might be writing to someone who has no idea why you are emailing them. I've too often received emails from strangers and sat there wondering what the purpose of this email was and what this person was trying to achieve by emailing me. So, ask yourself this: are you sure your point comes across sufficiently clearly for someone who doesn't know your project to understand what you are telling them?

Lastly, when proofreading your email aloud, ask yourself at what point in your email you might lose a potential recipient. Freedman and Fraser's research on compliance[20] shows that getting someone to agree to many small statements or questions increases the likelihood that they will say yes to a bigger question. For example, if your recipient agrees with each sentence in your email, they are more likely to positively respond to your email and act on your CTA. So, when proofreading your email, ask yourself if you are able to get a silent agreement from your recipient at each step of your email. Remember: the more they agree with your statements, the more likely they are to act.

Proofreading your email may not seem like a very exciting part of the writing process, but it is actually very important when emailing people you don't know or are calling to action. Keep their perspective in mind and always question whether your email accomplishes your goals.

CHAPTER THREE

Additional Content

The email text may be some people's main focus, whereas other people may want to also include content in different formats. For example, you might want to include a visual to illustrate your point or links to refer to your website. Whatever the context, you may be unsure of how these might affect your open, click, or response rates and feel stuck in your outreach.

Before you start adding any additional content to your emails, though, ask yourself how relevant that content is. The best practices below encourage adding different mediums to your outreach, but this does not mean they should be added automatically. Everything you include in an email should resonate with the recipient, and that goes for images, videos, and links too. Any content that is not relevant or interesting to the recipient would end up harming your email a lot more than if you had decided to stick to text only.

Regardless of the content you are sending, every part of your email should (a) add value to your message, placed purposefully to help illustrate what you are saying, and (b) illustrate only *the main idea* you are trying to convey. Your additional content, should you choose to add any, should be very relevant and sharp, emphasizing your point, rather than distracting from it.

In this chapter, you'll learn about best practices when incorporating images, videos, and links in your emails for maximum engagement.

Images

Perhaps the most common way of integrating content in an email is by adding images. Those can be charts, posters, pictures – anything to add some color to your words. But do these images help your engagement? Are people more likely to read, click, or respond if there is an image in the email?

As a general rule, images are much more likely to be remembered than text. This is called the Picture Superiority Effect.[21] In fact, we will mostly likely only remember 10% of the information presented in text. In contrast, when an image is presented with the text, we remember up to 65% of the information.

To best illustrate the impact of images, I ran the experiment myself and compared the performance of an email that included an image with one that did not.

The subject line and content were the exact same and these emails were all sent at the exact same time to avoid any conflicting variables. The only difference was the presence of an image versus no image.

The idea behind this email was to send a newsletter to our platform users. The first email contained the newsletter attached, while the second email showed the newsletter integrated with the text.

Over 20,000 emails were sent in total for each group.

For the first email, without the image, the open rate was 17% and the click rate 4%. Clearly there was room for improvement.

For the second email, with the image, the open rate was 17.75% – barely any different from the first email, which makes sense considering every aspect influencing the subject line was identical. The click rate, however, went up to 12.7%.

So, clearly adding an image encouraged people to click.

But are all images created equal or can we observe some differences in reactions depending on an image's presentation?

As you may have already guessed, colors in your images have a huge impact on how your message is received. According to color psychology, colors have the power to affect our emotions and determine how we feel about a specific product, brand, or message[22].

In fact, in 2011, HubSpot, the popular CRM tool, tested their color theory[23] by designing two web pages that were the same in every aspect – expect for one important detail: the CTA button color. On their first version of the page, the button was green, and on the second version, the same button was red.

Everything else on these webpages was the same, from font to graphics to text.

The results were very clear: the page with the red button outperformed the page with the green button by 21%.

Changing the color of the button had a great impact on people's likelihood to click on it.

Pick your color carefully depending on the emotion you are trying to elicit in your recipient, to ensure that you are communicating the right message. For example, according to User Testing[24], keep in mind these color concepts:

- red elicits excitement, strength, love
- orange elicits confidence, success, bravery
- yellow elicits creativity, happiness, warmth
- green elicits nature, healing, freshness
- blue elicits trust, peace, loyalty
- pink elicits compassion, sincerity, sophistication
- purple elicits royalty, luxury, ambition
- brown elicits dependable, rugged, simple
- black elicits formality, dramatic, security
- white elicits clean, simplicity, innocence

HOT TIP:
Check out Canva's interactive color wheel for more information on color choices.

However, keep in mind that not all email servers will be able to receive your images. Some companies have very strong security settings and automatically send image-heavy emails to spam. In addition, some servers may require users to enable images before they can see the images you send.

Unfortunately, there is no magic recipe when it comes to dodging spam filters. Every server will have different rules but, usually, the bigger the company, the stricter their rules are.

If you are looking to bypass these image spam filters, here are some recommendations:

1. Always include text in your email – sending an image alone raises red flags. Mailchimp recommends that you should keep a 20:80 image to text ratio in your email[25]
2. If you are emailing a large group of people, always include an unsubscribe link so people can unsubscribe instead of sending you directly to spam and thus creating red flags in their system.

Next time you are creating an email campaign, think strategically about how you can incorporate images in your email while avoiding the spam filter traps.

Video

Videos are quickly growing in popularity but still not used widely in emails. They are a great way to increase engagement in your emails, making you seem more human and real, and capture your recipient's full attention. According to Campaign Monitor[26], adding a video to an email boosts click-through rates by 65%, and reduces unsubscribes by 26% so, clearly, videos are a great way of engaging with people.

Like with any other type of content, though, you can never know for sure if someone is going to respond favorably to an email and while adding videos increases engagement, they can't guarantee it. Before sending a video, make sure that the person you are sending the video to will be receptive to this type of media: some people will be more receptive to creativity than others and it is important that you identify which group your recipient belongs to. Some considerations might be their age range, current activity, and content topic – the main question being: how likely is it that this person will click on the video and watch it?

There are many different types of videos you can include in your emails, but these are the most popular:

- Advertisement
- Platform demo video
- Introduction to yourself or your company/ product
- Industry updates
- Tutorials
- Case studies.

Videos are largely underutilized as email engagement tools so you will definitely stand out if you decide to incorporate a video. They help your recipient put a face to your name and confirm that you are not a robot.

They show creativity and presentation skills, and above all, they make it harder to ignore you. Just like they wouldn't ignore you if you were sitting in front of them, seeing your face talk to them will subconsciously encourage them to respond to you.

If you have decided to create video for your emails, here are some tips to help maximize your impact:

1. **Length**: according to Innovid, the CTV advertising and measurement platform, video length determines whether people video your ad until the end.[27] Their research shows that:

   a. 82.5% of people will view the entire ad if it lasts less than 10 seconds
   b. 85.9% of people will view the entire ad if it lasts 30 seconds
   c. 68.4% of people will view the entire ad if it lasts 60 seconds.

2. **Embed your video**: don't link your video, but rather embed it in your email so your recipient can see the preview and click directly on it in the email.
3. **Tools**: according to HubSpot's research surveying 550 marketers, 44% of them use an iPhone as their primary camera for filming videos,[28] so you don't necessarily need the fanciest equipment to get started.

Links

Last but definitely not least in our series of "extra content," let's dive into the impact links have on email engagement.

To illustrate the importance of including links in emails, Campaign Monitor, an email marketing software, conducted a study in 2019[29] on marketing emails specifically and found that unsubscribe rates declined when links were included in an email: emails with no links at all received "roughly 55% more unsubscribers than those with 1 or more links," noting that they excluded the unsubscribe link from the total number of links.

So, while we can all agree that including links in emails is important, and, in some cases, unavoidable, one important question remains: how many links is too many links?

Some people will tell you never to include more than three links, while others will tell you to add as many as you can. Of course, this depends on the nature of your email and the value each link brings to your email. But are there any general recommendations?

Campaign Monitor, in the same study, asked themselves this exact question and decided to test it out. They looked at over 500 million email recipients, analyzing their click rates and whether more links resulted in more clicks. And what they found contradicts quite beautifully the idea that less is more: according to their findings, more links resulted in a higher click rate, with an interesting peak in clicks at 14 links.

When it comes to links, people would rather have more choices to pick what they want to read, rather than having narrowed options. This means that the more information you add in your email, the more engaged people will become with what you are sharing and the more likely they are to look at what you are sending them.

It's of course important to note that these links do not have to be stand-alone links presented as bullet-points to your recipient. They can also be imbedded in your text and can, for example, include a link to your LinkedIn page, a link to your calendar for easy scheduling, a link to your company website, etc.

Taking their study one step further, Campaign Monitor then looked at how inserting unique URLs (the "ugly" part of the link, which usually starts with http or www) affected click rates and whether it was better to insert those rather than worded links.

Their results tell an unexpected story: including unique URLs, when possible, actually encouraged people to click more on the links than text-embedded links did.

This is because unique URLs allow the reader to see the source of the information, meaning that they can decide for themselves whether they consider this link trustworthy and important. People are very selective of how and where they receive information, so these unique URLs allow them to ensure that they are reading information valuable to them.

Lastly, the placement of your link in your email can also impact your click rate. A 2016 study on link placement in email newsletters shows that we scan newsletters in a U-shape pattern: from top-left to top-right of the page with click rate slowly decreasing as the eye scans the page.[30] This means that links placed in the top-left of the page are more likely to be clicked on than those in the top-right corner.

For your next email campaigns, I challenge you to use these best practices: diversify your email structure and consider the placement of your links to increase your chances of standing out in your recipient's inbox and impacting your results. However, of course, as always, use your better judgement in your email based on the specific context and content of your correspondence. Depending on the layout and structure of your email, these elements may be hard to incorporate, so take some time to reflect on the best link organization for your specific email.

Chapter Four

Email Personalization

As we saw in chapter 1, inserting the recipient's personal details can create a connection with them and make them feel targeted – not just another name on a list. This increases the likelihood of capturing their attention and receiving a response.

Many people agree that this personalization is necessary, but too many do not know where or how to start.

In this chapter, you will learn personalization best practices as well as how to tackle mass emails, where personalization seems so out of reach.

What Does Email Personalization Mean?

It involves including personal details about your recipient in your email. This can range from details about their role, their interests, their life... anything that is unique to them specifically.

Salesloft, the sales engagement platform, considers an email personalized when it is "significantly different from the original template." This means that if you are using email templates, your personalized email should contain enough personal details that it is "significantly" different from the original template.

Steve Richard, co-founder of the outsourced sales company Vorsight (now an Acquirent company), created a research method called the 3x3 method.[31] This consists of finding three pieces of contextual information about a person you are targeting in under three minutes.

The idea of the 3x3 Research is that you should not be spending hours researching each individual. Not only would that not be scalable in the business world, but it would also lead you down many unnecessary rabbit holes. Everything you need to know about the person you are reaching out to should be discoverable in three minutes.

In particular, there are three key types of details you should look for:

- **Personal:** promotions, career changes, social media engagement, personal interests
    - o   Search your recipient's LinkedIn profile – in particular, read their most recent posts for any info you could include in your email

- o Google your recipient for recent articles, podcasts, posts, etc.
- **Company:** leadership changes, press releases, strategy updates, product launches
  - o Search their company's LinkedIn page for any recent updates
  - o Google their company and check if they were in the news recently
  - o Check out their company's website for any information.
- **Industry:** effects of inflation, regulatory changes, new competitors
  - o Google their industry to find any updates and check the news.

Although the 3x3 Research was created specifically for sales prospecting, it's a great technique that can be replicated across many industries.

In addition to these three key details to look for, here are some examples of how you might contextualize and use this newly found information in your email:

- Include a quote or idea from an interview they gave
- Include a pain point they mention experiencing in a LinkedIn post

- Include a common interest you noticed
- Include a note about any recent changes in title or responsibilities
- Include something about their location – an event, the weather, etc.

To Personalize or Not to Personalize?

Salesloft ran a study[32] to decipher whether personalization was important in business emails. Looking at over 6 million sales emails, they found that personalizing 20% of the email content yielded an open rate increase of 40% and a reply rate increase of 112%.

This means that by adding a few thoughtful details about your recipient, you could skyrocket your open and response rates.

Personalization can completely overturn the outcome of an email. However, not all personalization is created equal.

While this may seem counter-intuitive in the business world, Salesloft found that when it comes to personalization, the more personal, the better.

Perhaps because these details create a deeper connection or perhaps because they show how much research you did on your recipient, these personal details yielded significantly better response and appointment setting rates than details related to their company or to current events:

Person-Specific Personalization Examples	Higher Response Rate	Higher Appointment Rate
Congratulating a promotion within the last 4 months	1.42x	2.29x
Congratulating achievement of a high position at a young age	1.99x	5.33x
Complimenting someone on recently being published	2.5x	4.53x
Sharing having gone to the same college	1.93x	1.82x
A landmark or famous place near childhood home	2.23x	7.21x
A baseball team someone is interested in	1.72x	3.84x
Having grown up in the same town	3.37x	8.79x

If you weren't convinced by the power of personalization before, hopefully you are now convinced and ready to try this out yourself.

> **HOT TIP:**
> Introduce these personal details early in your email (some time in the first paragraph) to encourage your recipient to continue reading.

How Do I Personalize a Mass Email?

There are infinite options when personalizing an individual email. You know who you are writing to, so you are easily able to research them and include personal details about them in your emails.

However, it's important to distinguish between individual emails sent to one specific person and mass emails sent to a large group of individuals.

Mass emails are a different ball game entirely. You are no longer addressing this email to one single individual, but rather to dozens, if not hundreds, of people at once.

There are several ways of personalizing mass emails, all sharing a similar concept: you need to segment the people you are emailing into specific groups. While you can't make your personalization individual-based, you can still find common traits between groups of people and use that as your in.

Here are some examples of effective segmentation for mass emails:

Segmentation	Explanation
Department	Segment your recipients based on their departments and mention a detail specific to their current projects
Geography	If you are reaching out to people spread across different countries, including details about your recipients' location is a great way to connect with them so use this as a segmentation idea
Prioritization	Decide who are the most important people in your list and pay closer attention to them – separate them from the rest of the group and personalize their emails
Pain Points	Different recipients may have different pain points you address, and your messaging may change across groups. Segment them based on these pain points to ensure maximum engagement
Personal Detail	Find similar interests among recipients to create a personal connection with a specific group

Most sales engagement platforms like Salesloft, Outreach, Marketo, FrontSpin, and more allow you to add dynamic fields that will auto-populate information based on the spreadsheet or CRM you connect to your platform.

For example, you can insert the "first name" dynamic field and it will populate your emails with all your recipient's first names before sending your emails. You can make these dynamic fields as simple or as complex as you'd like, depending on your personalization. However, always proofread your email before sending it off to ensure that the dynamic fields have been properly populated, to avoid miscalling someone or mentioning a detail about another person and confusing your recipient.

With these personalization tools, you will be able to pack a punch and open new doors to connections, conversations, and opportunities.

CHAPTER FIVE

Wording

Having looked at the content of your email, it's now important to work on wording. Many different parts of your email will affect your open, click, and response rates, and wording is one of them. The words you use in your email are very powerful and when used to your advantage, they can help maximize your email's engagement. However, poor language may lose your recipient's attention or dilute your message.

If you've been writing emails for a while, you've probably heard more than once that emails should be written as a third grader, or an eight-year-old, would – meaning a lot simpler than you would expect. While some may be skeptical, this is actually very good advice.

A study[33] led by Boomerang a few years ago compared response rates of emails written like a kindergartner, a third grader, a high school student, and a college student. While I would personally have thought that the college student level conveyed more credibility, people actually preferred to read simple emails with simple words written in an informal tone. In fact, college-level emails were the least successful of all four groups, with a 39% response rate, compared with 45% for high schoolers, 46% for kindergartners, and an impressive 53% for third graders.

If you have a tendency to overcomplicate your emails, using complex, impressive words, and mile-long sentences, ask yourself if a third grader would have been able to write your email. Let your inner child take the lead and simplify your vocabulary and sentence structure.

However, there are certain words that strengthen your emails, and others that dilute it. This chapter will take a closer look at what those words are and share best practices on email length.

Words to Use

When crafting your email, pay close attention to the words and phrases you are using. Make sure that the language you use is strong and precise, and conveys confidence and trust.

Below are some examples of words that will enhance
your message:

Words	Example	Why we like it
Thanks	Any opportunity you have to thank people	As seen earlier in the book when talking about sign-offs, people love gratitude. Of course, don't abuse this and thank your recipient at every sentence for no good purpose, but if there is an opportunity to thank them, take it. If they helped you out in any way, make sure they know how appreciative you are. You will sound warmer and more approachable.
!	What an exciting opportunity *!*	Controversial topic, but using exclamation points makes you sound more friendly, more personable, and less robotic. You will sound enthusiastic, and your recipient will feel the excitement. Don't abuse them, but if you feel like your sentence is exciting enough to warrant an exclamation point, embrace it!

Words	Example	Why we like it
		While some may worry that adding exclamation points makes you seem overly warm, research by AB Labs shows that using exclamation points in emails has little to no impact on how you are perceived.[34]
Because	Any sentence in the world that would use the word "because"	A 1978 Harvard study by Ellen Langer shows that using the word "because" when making a request increases the likelihood of getting a positive response by 55%.[35] The same applies in your emails – people like explanations. Use the word "because" and see your requests yield positive responses.
Let's	"*Let's* find some time to connect later this week"	When making plans, dividing tasks, talking about next steps, it's very important to show assertiveness. Using "let's" shows that you are taking the lead with confidence, thus encouraging people to trust and follow that lead.

Words	Example	Why we like it
Looking forward	*"Looking forward* to connecting tomorrow!"	This is especially true when booking meetings with people: show some excitement! People are going to be connecting with you so make sure you're conveying enthusiasm. If you're not looking forward to it, why should your recipient look forward to it?
You	Every chance you get	Your email should be about your recipient – everything you write should be aimed at them and how your services or product can help *them* so any chance you get, remind them that they are your first priority.
Power words	Replace non-power words with power ones whenever relevant throughout your email	Power words are used to illicit emotion in a reader. Often used by writers, academics, students, and more, they are a great way to strengthen your message. Many different lists exist but Capitalize My Title's list of "700+ Power Words to Use in Headlines, Resumes, and Email Subjects"[36] is my personal favorite.

Words Not to Use

In contrast, there are also words that diminish your message and weaken your point. Here are some examples of words not to use in your emails:

Words	Example	Why we avoid	Suggestion
Introducing yourself at the beginning of your email	"My name is Jane, and I am from Big Media Company"	This introduction is very impersonal and emphasizes that you have never spoken to this person before – remember, your first couple of words will appear in their inbox as the email preview, so make sure those words are inviting and warm. These will make you sound robotic and unoriginal.	Skip this introduction (they have your email signature for that) and jump straight into why you are emailing them.
Just	"*Just* checking in on the above"	Adding the word "just" dilutes the importance of your message and diminishes your confidence.	"Checking in on the above."

Words	Example	Why we avoid	Suggestion
I wanted to	"*I wanted to* follow up with you"	As Nike says, just do it – if you are writing this email, then you are past the point of *wanting to* do it, so just do it.	"Following up on my previous note."
I think / I was wondering	"I *think* it would be best to connect later this month" "I *was wondering* if you have also encountered this"	Thinking and wondering make you seem uncertain. Be more assertive, take your seat at the table, and make your recommendation with confidence. You know what you want so no need to wonder – be confident when introducing ideas or asking questions.	"Let's connect later this month." "Have you also encountered this?"
I hope this email finds you well	"*I hope this email finds you well*"	All variations of "hope you've been well" are bad, but this one is by far the worst.	Either ask them how they are and expect a response, or skip

Words	Example	Why we avoid	Suggestion
		While it's nice of you to wish your recipient well, it makes your email sound very generic and robotic, in addition to sounding very disingenuous.	this nicety altogether.
Sorry	"*Sorry* for not responding sooner"	While assuming blame is typically a positive trait after messing up, it tends not to be the case in emails. Apologizing emphasizes the error, thus adding a negative touch to the email and taking away from the real message you are conveying. Let's spin this in a more positive way!	"Thanks for your patience."

Words	Example	Why we avoid	Suggestion
Any generic phrase about what you or your product does that could be applied to any person or product	"Our product increases revenue and reduces costs"	So many business emails are filled with generic sentences like this one. Remember that you want to stand out from the lot and engage with your recipient so if you can't be more specific than that, you're not ready to send this email.	One sentence about how you or your product would make your recipient's life easier without using these clichéd and re-used sentences. Show your recipient that you have actually understood their pain points and that you, and no one else, fit their needs.

REMINDER HOT TIP:
Read your email out loud before pressing send – this will help you hear what your recipient will read and will ensure that you sound confident and natural.

Word Count

First impressions and what goes into those first judgements we place on a person have long been at the center of research. A 2017 study[37] found that it takes approximately 33ms or 0.033 seconds to decide whether a person is trustworthy.

While these findings were all based on facial expressions, the study shows that first impressions are drawn at record speed – and this is true for emails too. If we can judge a person's trustworthiness in 0.033 seconds just by looking at their face, how long do you think it takes people to judge the trustworthiness of your email? Probably even less than 0.033 seconds.

Being technologically connected at all times is great for so many reasons, but it also means that people will be reading your email in many different formats that you need to account for. Nowadays, and especially with the rise of remote work, people are not just reading emails at their desk, but also at the beach or while enjoying drinks with friends after hours. They're reading emails on their computers, but also on their phones and tablets. According to Litmus, in 2021, 42% of all emails were opened on a mobile device.[38] This means that your email needs to be easy to read and to skim on all platforms.

Moreover, the people you are reaching out to are all very busy, both at work and in their personal life. From the entry-level person to the CEO, reading and answering your email is probably not their priority so you need to maximize your chances of success every step of the way.

So, what does this mean for you? One of the main factors that will determine whether someone reaches the bottom of your email is its length – as seen on the computer as well as on their phone.

Think about all the times you've opened emails from strangers, not sure what to expect. How much time did you dedicate to that task? How many times did you exit an email or even delete it just because it was too long, and you didn't care enough to read all 500 words laid out in front of you? Be honest – we've all done this.

So, your task as the sender will be to remain in the category of people who send short, precise, and sharp emails, piquing your recipient's interest and curiosity.

Let's review two email examples:

Example #1 (word count: 202):
"Hi [name],

I noticed you are very involved with physical security and threat intel at [company] and was hoping I could talk with you about your current crisis management system.

We know that most organizations have an ENS in place to notify their employees and assets in the event of an emergency. However, the security executives we have been talking with have started focusing their attention towards being more proactive to threats rather than solely reactive, which I'm sure you'll agree, helps prevent catastrophes.

[My company] is a proactive security intelligence organization that works to alert clients of threats that are closest and most relevant to them. We deliver safety and security solutions that revolutionize how government and businesses collect, manage, share, and disseminate information to reduce cyber threats, fight crime, mitigate risks, manage incidents, and securely communicate and collaborate with one another. Aggregating and integrating information from public and private sources, [my company] leverages its cutting-edge technologies to bring users a highly customized presentation of relevant information in a single, easy to use solution.

Are you available sometime next week for a quick call about how you can become more proactive in the event of an emergency?

Thanks in advance,
[Name]"

Example #2 (word count: 106):
"Hi [name],

I understand you're very involved with physical security and threat intel at [company].

Law enforcement has always wanted to help companies stay on the front-end of emergencies but found that ENS and in-house analysts were reactive rather than proactive. This led to companies reacting too late to threats once security was already jeopardized. This is why they came to us: to ensure that organizations remain proactive in the event of an emergency.

Let's chat about what companies are doing to remain proactive and our work with law enforcement. What does your calendar look like next week for a quick call?

Thanks in advance,
[Name]"

Which of these emails do you think was most successful? Which one stands out most in an executive's inbox? Which one are they most likely to read because it requires less time to go through and to understand the message? Which one is more succinct and direct?

The second one, of course!

Keep in mind that the executives you are emailing receive hundreds of emails per day. Some are relevant. But most aren't. And executives aren't going to spend 10 minutes per email. They will spend one to two minutes – at most.

To stand out, your emails need to be short, concise, and to the point, illustrating the idea that you are not there to waste their time. In fact, you're there to save them time with your company's awesome product or service. Shorter emails are much more likely to get read than longer ones.

In fact, Boomerang did a study[39] a few years back on how long business emails should be. According to them, emails between 50 and 125 words – most likely a lot shorter than the emails you are currently writing – get "response rates above 50%."

The table below summarizes their findings:

Number of Words in Email	Response Rate
10 Words	36%
25 Words	44%
50 Words	50%
75 Words	**51%**
100 Words	**51%**
125 Words	50%
150 Words	49%
175 Words	49%
200 Words	48%

Next time you are writing an email, pay close attention to the words you are using and how you can maximize your ~100 words. Delete the fluff and remain engaging!

HOT TIP #1:
Send yourself a preview of your email and review it both on your computer and on your phone. Double check for any formatting or length issues before sending it to your intended recipient.

HOT TIP #2:
Write your email as you usually would, without paying attention to the word count, and once you have a full email, go back and trim sentences to shrink it to 50–125 words. Delete filler words and fluff so that only the sharpest, most relevant parts of your email remain.

CHAPTER SIX

Timing

Your email is now written, proofread, and ready to be sent out. One question still remains: when should you send it?

According to Statista, the consumer data company, over 300 **billion** emails were sent and delivered in 2020 and that number is predicted to continue to rise.[40] An astonishingly high number, although I can't say I'm surprised. We use emails all day, every day in our business communications – hence the importance of being strategic.

With so many emails sent and delivered each day, it's very easy for them to get lost in your recipient's inbox – unless you are strategic about your timing and maximize your chances of success!

When it comes to timing, everyone has an opinion – some will advise you to send your most important emails on Mondays because that's when people create their to-do lists for the week; some will tell you to avoid afternoons because those are popular meeting times so your email will get lost... So many differing opinions and advice.

But what does the data tell us?

This chapter looks in detail at which time of the day and day of the week lead to the highest open, click, and response rates, as well as best practices for handling out-of-office replies.

Time of Day

The most common advice about timing tends to be that mornings and lunch times are best. These moments are when people are either starting their day and checking their inbox first thing in the morning or enjoying a lunch break and catching up on any emails in between meetings.

While this is not necessarily bad advice, it is missing important aspects of the story.

When you are sending emails and hoping for engagement, it's important you ask yourself what type of engagement you are after – opens, clicks, or responses.

The best time of day to send an email will be different depending on your desired outcome.

Looking at almost 2,000,000 emails sent in Salesloft, sent at various times across all days of the week with different purposes, and to different personas across several industries, I was able to gather insights into timing best practices.

Keep in mind that these statistics are averages spanning many industries, so the data may look slightly different from one to another. But as you can see in the graph below, if you are looking to increase your **open rate**, mornings are a great time to reach out. Lunch time, in contrast, has one of the lowest open rates of the day. If your emails aren't sent early morning, you might as well wait until mid to late afternoon, around 3pm, when open rates spike up again.

If the purpose of your email is to increase your **click** rate, the best time to send emails is during this infamous lunch time, right when open rates are low. You may have fewer people opening your emails, but those that are opening them are more likely to click on your content.

If you are trying to increase your **response** rate, afternoons, especially around 3pm, offer you the highest likelihood of a reply.

Given that timings for open, click, and response rates vary, it's hard to pinpoint one significantly better time to send your emails to maximize impact on all three metrics. Before sending your email, ask yourself which of these three elements is most important to you.

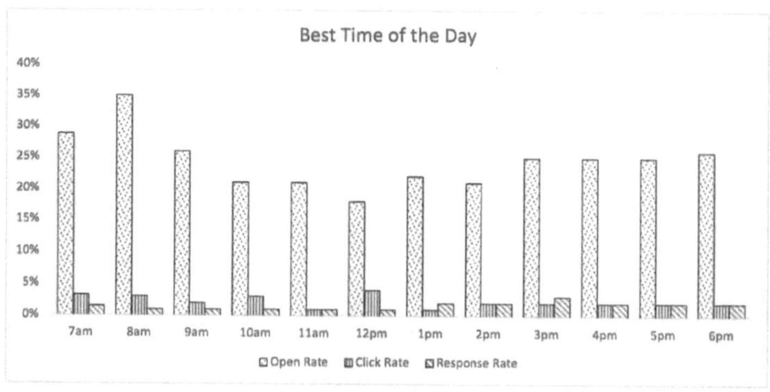

Source: Salesloft Analytics

HOT TIP:
Email people 5–10 minutes before the hour to increase your chances of getting a response. Your recipient will likely be in between meetings and checking their emails to fill the awkward time before their next meeting, when they don't have enough time to start a task, but have too much time to wait idly.

Day of the Week

Similarly to the time of day, deciding which day of the week to email someone also depends on the purpose of your email. Open, click, and response rates show significant differences depending on the day you send your email.

If your goal is to increase your **open** rate, it is recommended that you send your email on Wednesday, and definitely not on Thursday. Motivation and productivity tend to slow on Wednesdays as we head into the latter part of the week and people are more tempted to spend more time sending emails. Thursday, on the contrary, tends to be a meeting-heavy day for many people as they pack their agenda for a lighter Friday, leaving less time for emails.

If you are looking to increase your **click** rate, Wednesday now becomes the worst day to send your emails, and Monday and Thursday become your best bets, when productivity are high and people are motivated to not only read emails to pass time, but take action on what they read.

If you are looking for a high **response** rate, Tuesday is the best-performing day and yields the highest number of responses.

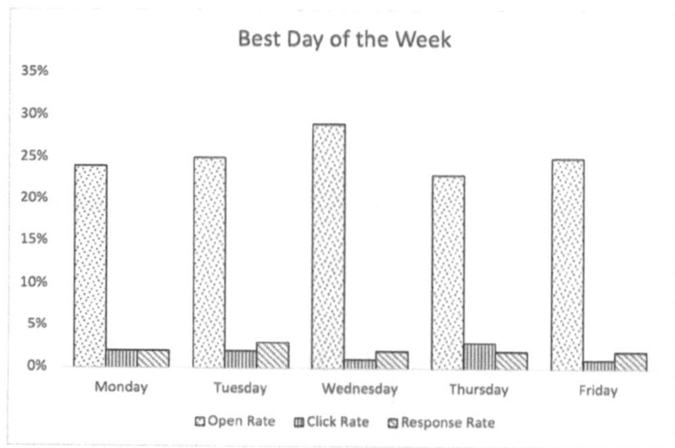

Source: Salesloft Analytics

If we connect the dots and interpret the data we just looked at, we can see that depending on what the goal of your cadence is, you will need to send it at different times and on different days.

To summarize:

- Best moment to send a cadence for the highest **open rate:** *Wednesday at 8am*
- Best moment to send a cadence for the highest **click rate:** *Thursday at 12 noon*
- Best moment to send a cadence for the highest **response rate:** *Tuesday at 3pm*

Using this information will empower you to make the smartest decisions and time your emails at the moment most likely to help you in your endeavor.

Out-of-Office Replies

A common pain point in the business world, we often send very important emails but are met with a disappointing out-of-office reply. If you've ever sent mass emails, you might even have been on the receiving end of several hundred automated emails flooding your inbox.

What should you do with these automatic replies? Should you simply ignore them? Should you store them? Should you make a note of people's return date?

These are all great questions with answers that vary depending on the nature of your email and the number of automated responses you are receiving.

Before you proceed, check with your manager or co-workers whether your company has any specific policies regarding these emails, or ask yourself if you would like to handle these in any specific way. Some companies make note of them in their CRM while others ignore them completely. In addition, always make sure that you are complying with local data protection regulations and regulations that apply to your business and where you are located, as well as where your recipient is located. For example, the EU's General Data Protection Regulation (GDPR) limits data collection from all people located in the EU, regardless of where you are based.

While I will always discourage you from reaching out to people you know are away for the sake of information, out-of-office replies can give a generous amount of details to those who are looking. Here are some best practices on how to handle out-of-office responses:

Response	How to handle it
They are no longer at the company	Update your list or CRM to reflect the change and look up where they now work – this person could still be a lead but at a different company
They are on extended leave (parental leave, summer vacation, etc.)	Remove this contact from your cadence while they are away and make a note of their return date.
	Once they are back, send them a welcome back note – these are always appreciated, personalize your email, and show that you paid attention.

Response	How to handle it
They included an alternate way of reaching them (a cell phone number, for example)	Include this new information in your list or CRM. If applicable and appropriate, use this info to continue your outreach. ⚠ Make sure you are respecting people's time and boundaries. If they included information in their automated response, there is a high chance they are open to the outreach, but always be mindful of your contact's space.
There is someone else's contact information in the automatic response	Make a note of that person's information, look them up, and if they fit the persona you are searching for or could have helpful information, contact them. Make sure to include that you were sent their way via someone's out-of-office reply. Great icebreaker and reason to email someone! They may be able to help you while your desired recipient is out.
You receive an overwhelming number of automated responses	Store them in a separate folder and sort through them when you have time using the best practices in the rows above. You will most likely never get through all of them, and that's okay – what matters most is that they do not clog your inbox and you slowly update your list or CRM for contacts who are no longer at the company.

Lastly, don't hesitate to respond to out-of-office messages that spoke to you. While it may not be the best idea if someone is out for several months (imagine their inbox on their return!), it would be a nice touch for someone who's out for only a few days.

If you find their automated response particularly funny, they mention an amazing vacation, etc., drop them a note of support! Including this detail in their out-of-office shows that it is important to them so don't miss an opportunity to create a connection with them.

For example, it can be as simple as:

"Hey [first name],

I've always wanted to visit Iceland – sounds like an incredible vacation and I hope you enjoy every second of it! I'll give you a call when you're back in the office but in the interest of not catching you when you're busy, feel free to use the link in my signature to book some time.

Thanks,
[Name]"

You won't always get an answer, but the times you do will make this technique worth it. You will seem more human (a bot would definitely not have written that!), more compassionate, and more genuine in your outreach.

CHAPTER SEVEN

Follow-Ups

Have you ever noticed that the more you hear a song, the more you start to like it? The first time you heard that melody, you didn't really vibe with it and paid little attention to it. But then, the more you heard it on the radio, the more you started to like it, until eventually, you were obsessed with it.

Or have you ever bought a product from a certain brand just because the name sounded familiar, or because you recognized the logo?

This phenomenon is called the mere exposure effect.[41] The original study, which has now been replicated with many different stimuli, looks at a group of participants' reactions to neutral images. Some people were exposed to the images only one time, some several times, and others up to 25 times. The results showed that the more people were exposed to these images, the more they reported liking them.

Why am I telling you about images? Because this mere exposure effect plays in our favor when thinking about email strategies. Just like images, the more people see your name, your company logo, your company name, etc., the more familiar they become with that and the more likely they are to like you.

This mere exposure effect is one of the drivers of follow-up emails because it predicts that the more follow-up emails you send, the higher the chances of success.

In this chapter, you will learn more about why follow-up emails are crucial to your email strategy and how you can pack a punch when writing yours.

Why Are Follow-Up Emails Important?

On average, it takes around eight contacts[42] (email, voicemail, call, etc.) to schedule a meeting with someone you don't personally know. That's right – eight times!

Yet, according to every research out there and almost every single person I've ever spoken with, most business professionals will stop their outreach after one or two touches. In sales specifically, an overwhelming majority of professionals will give up if they do not receive a response after their first attempt.

So where is the disconnect?

The most common answer is that we consider silence to be a "no." For example, in life, if the girl you are trying to ask out ignores you, you interpret that as a negative answer and move on.

However, in the business world, silence does not always mean no. For example, silence can mean that your email got lost in your recipient's inbox and they never read it. Silence can mean that your recipient read your email and meant to respond but an urgent project got added to their workload and they forgot. Silence can mean that your email got caught in a spam filter and was never received.

Silence does not mean that you should stop reaching out and in the three examples outlined above, the only way to remain top of mind is for you to follow up. Not receiving a response does not necessarily mean that your recipient is not interested in what you sent, but (perhaps) merely that they have not yet voiced that interest.

The second reason so few people send follow-ups is that many simply don't think about it. So much energy is spent crafting that first email that we start to see this process as a one-step done deal. After sending the email, we move on to a different task and forget about this one altogether until we look at our results and wonder why they weren't more positive.

Lastly, many people don't follow up simply because they don't know what to say. The person obviously hasn't responded yet, so what can they say that will make their recipient react the second time around?

What Should Your Follow-Ups Say?

There are two different types of follow-up emails: the simple reminder and the value-adder.

The simple reminder acts, as its name suggests, only as a reminder and should only be about two lines long. This follow-up assumes that your recipient merely forgot to respond, and a generic reminder will suffice to get an answer.

It usually looks something like this: "Popping this message back to the top of your inbox. [insert CTA.]"

The value-adder is much longer and provides the recipient with additional context and information on the purpose of your outreach. It might include more links, a video, an image, a story, an attached informational one-sheeter – anything to provide more value. This follow-up assumes that your recipient did not yet respond because they are not convinced about the value of what you are presenting to them and need some more convincing.

Here are some ideas to include if you are sending a value-adder follow-up:

- Use case
- Successful project
- Examples of previous work
- Video explaining who you are and how you work
- References or positive feedback you've received for your work
- Objection handling: address any doubts or questions you think they might have that prevent them from positively answering.

Regardless of which follow-up email type you decide to send to your recipient, make sure that your call to action is re-iterated in strong, clear language. Now that you have a second chance of capturing their attention, use it wisely!

Lastly, your follow-up emails should incorporate the best practices we looked at in previous chapters, meaning that you should remain conscious of timing, personalization, word count, and more.

How Many Follow-Ups Should You Send?

Now that we've established how crucial these follow-ups are, it's important to look at how many follow-ups you should be sending. In general, you want to send enough that your recipient sees enough value and eventually responds.

However, a common concern is that you will anger this person and lose your shot. As we saw, people receive so many emails every day – should we really be adding to that number?

When sending emails, always keep your audience in mind and use your better judgement – not every email should have a follow-up. Depending on the purpose of your email and your recipient, you may want to stick to one email only. However, data shows that the more follow-ups you send, the more responses you will receive.

Moreover, not only should you be sending follow-ups, but you should be sending *several* follow-ups!

In 2021, Yesware conducted a study[43] looking at over 10 million email threads. They looked specifically at sales threads, but the data they found can be applied to almost any industry and situation.

According to them, for best results, follow-ups should be sent roughly four days apart and "the most successful cadence based on replies is six touches in the span of roughly three weeks."

This means that next time you are crafting your cadence, make sure to add roughly five follow-ups after your original email to maximize your chances of getting a reply.

Beware – we do have one exception to this rule. We previously looked at the mere exposure effect, which suggests that the more we are exposed to a stimulus, the more likely we are to like that stimulus. However, research shows that this cannot work if there were pre-existing negative feelings about the stimulus.[44]

This means that sending follow-up emails would greatly annoy those who did not like you, your product, or your company to begin with. The more exposed to you they are, the greater the negative feelings will be, probably resulting in negative results such as angry emails or the loss of a customer.

When planning out your cadence and follow-up emails, ensure as far as possible that you are not following up with anyone who already has negative feelings about you or your company, or you may do more damage than good.

How Far Apart Should I Schedule My Follow-Ups?

When sending follow-up emails, it is crucial to send them in an organized and structured way. Sending emails too close together might annoy your recipient but sending them too far apart might weaken your message.

Interestingly, researchers Farshad Kooti and Kristina Lerman studied over 16 billion emails over several months and found that of all responses sent, 90% of those responses are sent on the day the email is received.[45] If you are not receiving responses, it is acceptable to follow up within two or three days to ensure that you remain top of mind.

In fact, in Yesware's study on email follow-ups, they found that waiting more than four days in between follow-ups significantly decreased the likelihood of receiving a response.

That being said, there are instances where you may want to leave more or less time between steps. Follow-ups should be strategically planned out, and depending on the nature of your cadence, the emotion you are trying to convey, the urgency of your ask, your touch plan will look very different.

Let's look at some of the most successful touch plans I've come across in the past to inspire your next cadence.

Note: the counting of days includes weekends.

Rushed Touch Plan

<table>
<tr><td>Purpose: you are in a rush to get an answer so emphasize the beginning of the touch plan to receive an answer as fast as possible</td></tr>
<tr><td>Length: 90 days</td></tr>
<tr><td>Day 1: first email
Day 3: first email reminder
Day 5: first email reminder #2
Day 10: added value
Day 17: added value #2
Day 31: added value #3
Day 60: is now a better time?
Day 90: break-up email</td></tr>
</table>

Urgency Touch Plan[46]

<table>
<tr><td>Purpose: you are willing to wait for an answer but want to drive urgency in the person right as they start to pay attention to you</td></tr>
<tr><td>Length: 30 days</td></tr>
<tr><td>Day 1: first email
Day 15: first email reminder
Day 22: added value #1
Day 26: added value #2
Day 28: added value #3
Day 29: when would be a better time?
Day 30: break-up email</td></tr>
</table>

First Intro Touch Plan

Purpose: you are reaching out to people who have no idea what you do and you are introducing the product to them
Length: 22 days
Day 1: first email (no CTA) Day 3: added value and first CTA Day 8: added value and previous CTA follow-up Day 15: is my timing bad? (include CTA) Day 22: added value and parting words (no CTA)

Nurture Touch Plan

Purpose: you want to make sure your products and services are regularly flagged to the reader, but you don't necessarily need an answer any time soon
Length: however long you want it to last
One email per month for as long as you want the cadence to last

HOT TIP:
These touch plan examples only show the email part of the cadence – each one should incorporate calls, voicemails, LinkedIn outreach, etc. in addition to these emails.

Chapter Eight

Reactions

When emailing people you don't necessarily know well – or at all – and asking them to do something specific, you are bound to receive various types of responses. You will see the first responses trickle into your inbox and feel so much excitement at what doors might be opening.

However, you'll quickly notice that there are as many reactions as there are recipients. Some people will be particularly receptive to emails and curious about what you have to offer them, while others won't be quite as enthused.

Send enough emails and you will be able to create your own library of reactions – some that will make you actually laugh out loud, and some that will make you want to un-send every single email you have ever sent. Those positive ones will be easy to handle, but the negative ones can be quite tricky.

However, no matter how harsh some responses might seem, remember that negative reactions aren't always about you. Some people will get angry at your outreach, but that does not mean that they are mad at you or that you should stop your efforts. Try not to take these reactions personally and remember that you are only doing your job. You will never be able to control other people's reactions or emotions, so keep doing your best and results will follow.

For every rude email you receive, there are dozens of positive ones finding their way to you.

In this chapter, we will look at different types of email reactions and you will learn more about how to handle each of them.

Examples and How to Handle Them

Emotion	Examples	How to handle it
Uninterested	<ul><li>"Unsubscribe"</li><li>"Please take me off your list"</li><li>"STOP"</li><li>"Not interested"</li></ul>	Uninterested people will most likely make up the largest portion of responses you receive. These reactions put you in a very interesting position: you can either take them off your list, update your CRM

Emotion	Examples	How to handle it
		accordingly, and never think about them every again, or take the path less traveled on and try again. Sometimes clarifying your original email is enough to make them change their mind. But make sure you are being considerate of the fact that they asked you to stop emailing them. Acknowledge that, apologize for insisting, and clarify what you were saying. I've done this several times and have either gotten ignored (no big deal) or gotten exactly what I wanted.
Wrong person	• "I'm not who you're looking for" • "Not my role"	First and foremost, update your CRM to make sure you stop emailing them, but once that's done, always remember to ask them who the correct person is, if they didn't offer you a name already. Depending on their company's size, structure, hierarchy, and job titles, it may be almost impossible for you to find the correct person without some internal help and this person gave you an in.

Emotion	Examples	How to handle it
Nice	• "Awesome [name], thank you so much! My apologies for the delay to answer, I was literally using your material to finish the QBR hehe. Thanks again and have a great weekend" • "Fantastic! Thank you so much!" • "Keep up the great work" • "Excellent email!"	For all the mean and rude emails you'll receive, don't forget to appreciate the kind ones! These outweigh the bad ones, by far, making what we do worth every rude comment we get. Thank them for their email and their kindness and make sure to stay in touch with them. These people could very possibly become your biggest advocates.
Helpful (maybe?)	• "Your original email is way too long. There's too much there. Be succinct, direct, and tell me how your platform will benefit me. What's the business value? Both to me and the organization I work for." • "Instead of wasting my time, go join a real cause and join the current protests going on in the US" (followed by a very long list of resources)	Some people want to be kind and give us feedback, but oftentimes, this is coming from people who have no clue what we do or how to do it. These will (usually) come from well-meaning people who took the time to help you out. Thank them for their time, bond with them, take their advice into consideration when answering them, and try your CTA again. Who knows, maybe they just need another nudge.

Emotion	Examples	How to handle it
Angry	<ul><li>"Rot and die! How dare you send spam to the entire workforce! Get a life!"</li><li>"Let me tell you that your professional persistence is the equivalent of a wily fly you just can't smash no matter how many times you try"</li><li>"Only scammers are this annoying"</li><li>"Wow you're spamming me hard. You're wasting my time"</li><li>"I would be surprised if this 'cold call' technique is successful for you or your organization"</li></ul>	Some people get particularly angry when receiving emails. Trust me when I say that most of the time, it has nothing to do with you. That person is probably just having a bad day, or you're the 10th cold email in a row landing in their inbox. Regardless of what the reason is, don't let that faze you. Apologize, delete them from your list, and move on to the next person you're reaching out to. No matter how beautifully crafted and perfectly on point your emails are, you will never be able to avoid negative reactions. Don't let that bring you down or discourage you from sending your follow-ups and continuing the course.

These reactions to your emails, no matter how rude they may be, do mean that your recipient not only opened your emailed, but also took time to respond to it. That's a win! Use this data to refine your target audience to avoid emailing the wrong people next time.

While a positive response is always better than an insult, the fact that someone took time out of their day to respond is not insignificant – something about your email triggered a reaction in them. And if nothing else, at least you know your subject line worked!

Conclusion

I hope that this book will guide you through all the decisions needed to make while writing emails and will ensure that you put all chances on your side when you are emailing, regardless of the type of email you are sending.

In a world that is becoming more virtual every day, we have started to rely on these email correspondences for just about everything we do, and emails have become a crucial part of every professional's career. With the number of emails we all receive each day, we are easily inundated with information and it is not always clear what or whom we should be paying attention to. From conversations with clients, co-workers, prospective employers, we use emails constantly, and it is crucial to understand and to master how to stand out in your recipients' inboxes.

I hope this book will guide you towards value-driven communication and will enhance the place emails play in our daily life. By upgrading the way we correspond, it is my wish that inboxes will no longer be filled with vague, unnecessary emails, but rather with poignant, relevant, and interesting ones we want to engage with.

As we have seen throughout this book, to distinguish yourself from all other people working to capture your recipient's attention, you need to work on every single aspect of your email. Every part of it plays a role in maximizing your chances of being seen, read, and actioned upon by your recipient. From your subject line to your email signature to the number of links you include in your email, every detail is important and different ways of presenting information lead to different outcomes.

The appendix of this book is presented as a checklist summarizing everything we have reviewed in these pages to ensure you have an easy-access guide to the elements that will help you catch anyone's attention.

Now grab your keyboard and get to writing!

APPENDIX

Email Checklist

Now that we've reviewed all the different parts of a business email and what differentiates the good from the great, let's make sure you have all the elements together!

Check this list before sending your emails to ensure maximum success:

Subject Line	☐ Does your subject line evoke an emotion in your reader? ☐ Is your subject line less than 7 words long? ☐ Is your subject line related to your email's main point? ☐ If applicable, does it include personalization? ☐ If applicable, does it include a question?
Greeting	☐ Does your email have a greeting that conveys the tone you are expressing?

Body	☐ Does your first paragraph clearly state the reason you are emailing *them*?
	o If applicable, did you include pre-call research?
	☐ Is your second paragraph centered around your product/service/main idea?
	o Does it tell a story? o Does it focus on why your company/product/main idea exists?
	☐ Is your third paragraph (your CTA) structured in two parts?

	o Part 1: a summary of what you said in your email
	    o Part 2: the actual CTA
	    o Do you only have one CTA in your email?

Sign-Off	☐ If applicable, does your sign-off express gratitude? ☐ Do you have a clean email signature with your name, title, email address, phone number, and company name and logo?

Content	☐ Is your email between 50 and 125 words? ☐ If you have images, are they emphasizing your main point? ☐ If you have images, do you have text included in your email that represents 80% of the content? ☐ If you have videos, do they present your point in a creative and engaging way? ☐ If you have links, are they all constructive and do they add to your main point?
Personalization	☐ If your email is personalized, does the personalization add to your main point?
Timing	☐ Are you sending your email at a time and date that maximizes what you are hoping to achieve (open rate, click rate, response rate)?
Follow-Ups	☐ Do you have follow-up emails planned out strategically? ☐ If applicable, do your follow-up emails add value to your main idea from your first email?

Final Re-read	<ul><li>☐ Have you proofread your email out loud to yourself?</li><li>☐ Has someone else external to your project read your email and given you feedback?</li><li>☐ Are you confident that your email is clear and that your recipient will understand why you are emailing them?</li></ul>

References

1 Chui, M., Manyika, J., Bughin, J., Dobbs, R., Roxburgh, C., Sarrazin, H., Sands, G., & Westergren, M. (2012). (rep.). *The Social Economy: Unlocking Value and Productivity through Social Technologies.* McKinsey Global Institute. Retrieved 2022, from https://www. mckinsey.com/~/media/mckinsey/industries/technology %20media%20and%20telecommunications/high%20 tech/our%20insights/the%20social%20economy/mgi_ the_social_economy_full_report.pdf.

2 Campaign Monitor. (2022). (rep.). *Ultimate Email Benchmarks for 2022: By Industry and Day.* Retrieved 2022, from https://www.campaignmonitor.com/resources/ guides/email-marketing-benchmarks/.

3 Campaign Monitor. (2022). (rep.). *Ultimate Email Benchmarks for 2022: By Industry and Day.* Retrieved 2022, from https://www.campaignmonitor.com/resources/ guides/email-marketing-benchmarks/.

4 Macdonald, S. (2022). *The Science Behind Email Open Rates (And How To Get More People To Read your Emails).* SuperOffice. Retrieved 2022, from https://www. superoffice.com/blog/email-open-rates.

5 Kahneman, D., & Tversky, A. (1979). Prospect Theory: An Analysis of Decision under Risk. *Econometrica*, 47(2), 263–291. https://doi.org/10.2307/1914185.

6 Guadagno, R. E., & Cialdini, R. B. (2010). Preference for consistency and social influence: A review of current research findings. *Social Influence, 5*(3). 152–163. https://doi.org/10.1080/15534510903332373

7 Experian. (2014). *2013 Email Market Study*

8 Madden, M. (2018). *What Email Subject Line Length Works Best?* Marketo Marketing Blog.

9 *10 Subject Line Tips to Incerase Your Email Open Rates in Sales*. (2019). Salesloft. https://salesloft.com/resources/blog/10-subject-line-tips-increase-open-rates/

10 Keohane, J. (2021). *Email Subject Lines: 10 Data-Backed Ways to Boost Open Rates (+Examples)*. Yesware. Retrieved 2022, from https://www.yesware.com/blog/email-subject-lines.

11 Williams, M. (2018). *How To Avoid Spam Filters When Sending Emails*. Yesware. Retrieved 2022, from https://www.yesware.com/blog/email-spam.

12 Greenley, B. (2018). *How to Start an Email: An Email Openings Analysis of 300,000+ Messages*. Quartz. Retrieved 2022, from https://qz.com/work/1184551/how-to-start-an-email-an-email-openings-analysis-of-300000-messages.

13 Sinek, S. (2009). *How Great Leaders Inspire Action*. TEDxPuget Sound. https://www.ted.com/talks/simon_sinek_how_great_leaders_inspire_action?language=en#t-139092.

14 Reed, D. (2020, May 27). *This (Surprising) Cold Email CTA Will Help You Book A LOT More Meetings*. Gong

Labs. https://www.gong.io/blog/this-surprising-cold-email-cta-will-help-you-book-a-lot-more-meetings.

15 Aland, M. C. (2021). *This Scheduling Hack Will 3x Your Chances of a Booked Meeting*. Chili Piper. https://www.chilipiper.com/resources/hub/3x-booked-meetings.

16 Murdock, B. B., Jr. (1962). The serial position effect of free recall. *Journal of Experimental Psychology, 64*(5), 482–488. https://doi.org/10.1037/h0045106.

17 Greenley, B. (2017). *Forget "Best" or "Sincerely," This Email Closing Gets the Most Replies*. Boomerang. https://blog.boomerangapp.com/2017/01/how-to-end-an-email-email-sign-offs/#footnotes.

18 Grant, A. M., & Gino, F. (2010). A little thanks goes a long way: Explaining why gratitude expressions motivate prosocial behavior. *Journal of Personality and Social Psychology, 98*(6), 946–955. https://doi.org/10.1037/a0017935.

19 Cushing, C., & Bodner, G. E. (2022). Reading aloud improves proofreading (but using Sans Forgetica font does not). *Journal of Applied Research in Memory and Cognition, 11*(3), 427–436. https://doi.org/10.1037/mac0000011.

20 Freedman, J. L., & Fraser, S. C. (1966). Compliance without pressure: The foot-in-the-door technique. *Journal of Personality and Social Psychology, 4*(2), 195–202. https://doi.org/10.1037/h0023552.

21 McBride, D. M., & Dosher, B. A. (2002). A Comparison of Conscious and Automatic Memory Processes for Picture and Word Stimuli: A Process Dissociation

Analysis. *Consciousness and Cognition*, 11(3), 423–460. https://doi.org/10.1016/s1053-8100(02)00007-7.

22 Elliot, A. J., & Maier, M. A. (2014). Color Psychology: Effects of Perceiving Color on Psychological Functioning in Humans. *Annual Review of Psychology*, 65(1), 95–120. https://doi.org/10.1146/annurev-psych-010213-115035.

23 Porter, J. (2017). *The Button Color A/B test: Red Beats Green*. HubSpot Blog. Retrieved 2022, from https://blog.hubspot.com/blog/tabid/6307/bid/20566/the-button-color-a-b-test-red-beats-green.aspx.

24 *How color impacts conversion rates and UX*. UserTesting. (2019). Retrieved 2022, from https://www.usertesting.com/blog/color-ux-conversion-rates#testing.

25 *Common HTML Mistakes*. Mailchimp. Retrieved 2022, from https://mailchimp.com/help/common-html-mistakes.

26 *How to Use Video in Your Email Marketing*. Campaign Monitor. Retrieved 2022, from https://www.campaignmonitor.com/resources/guides/video-in-email.

27 Innovid. (2022). (rep.) *A New Era of Personalization: Global Video Benchmarks Report*.

28 Lestraundra, A. (2022). *50 Video Marketing Statistics to Inform Your 2022 Strategy [New Data]*. HubSpot Blog. Retrieved 2022, from https://blog.hubspot.com/marketing/video-marketing-statistics.

29 Hodgekiss, R. (2019). *Do Fewer Links Mean More Clicks? (2019 Update)*. Campaign Monitor. https://www.campaignmonitor.com/blog/email-marketing/less-links-are-better.

30 Kumar, A., & Salo, J. (2016). Effects of link placements in email newsletters on their click-through rate, *Journal of Marketing Communications*, 24(5), 535-548. https://doi.org/10.1080/13527266.2016.1147485

31 *3x3 Research*, created by Steve Richard, co-founder of Vorsight (now an Acquirent company).

32 *Everything You Need To Know About Sales Email Personalization*. (2018). Salesloft. https://salesloft.com/resources/guide/sales-email-personalization.

33 Moore, A. (2016). *7 Tips for Getting More Responses to Your Emails (With Data!)*. Boomerang. https://blog.boomerangapp.com/2016/02/7-tips-for-getting-more-responses-to-your-emails-with-data.

34 *Emails & Exclamation Marks – Do They Affect Your Image?* AB Lab. https://www.ab-lab.org/emails-and-exclamation-marks.html.

35 Langer, E., Blank, A., & Chanowitz, B. (1978). The Mindlessness of Ostensibly Thoughtful Action: The Role of 'Placebic' Information in Interpersonal Interaction. *Journal of Personality and Social Psychology, 36(6),* 635–642. https://doi.org/10.1037/0022-3514.36.6.635.

36 Capitalize My Title. (2021). *700+ power Words to Use in Headlines, Resumes, and Email Subjects*. https://capitalizemytitle.com/power-words-to-use-in-headlines-and-email-subjects.

37 South Palomares, J. K., & Young, A. W. (2018). Facial First Impressions of Partner Preference Traits: Trustworthiness, Status, and Attractiveness. *Social Psychological and Personality Science, 9(8),* 990–1000. https://doi.org/10.1177/1948550617732388.

38 *Litmus. (2021). 2021 Email Client Market Share.*

39   Moore, A. (2016). *7 Tips for Getting More Responses to Your Emails (With Data!)*. Boomerang. https://blog.boomerangapp.com/2016/02/7-tips-for-getting-more-responses-to-your-emails-with-data.

40   Johnson, J. (2021). *Number of Sent and Received E-Mails Per Day Worldwide from 2017 to 2025*. Statista. https://www.statista.com/statistics/456500/daily-number-of-e-mails-worldwide.

41   Zajonc, R. B. (1968). Attitudinal effects of Mere Exposure. *Journal of Personality and Social Psychology, 9*(2, Pt.2), 1–27. https://doi.org/10.1037/h0025848.

42   Schultz, M. (2018). *How Many Touches Does It Take To Make A Sale?* https://www.rainsalestraining.com/blog/how-many-touches-does-it-take-to-make-a-sale

43   Keohane, J. (2021). *Number of Times to Follow Up & Cadence*. Yesware. https://www.yesware.com/blog/sales-follow-up-statistics/#number-of-times-to-follow-up.

44   Swap, W. C. (1977). Interpersonal Attraction and Repeated Exposure to Rewarders and Punishers. *Personality and Social Psychology Bulletin, 3*(2), 248–251. https://doi.org/10.1177/014616727700300219.

45   Kooti, F., Aiello, L., Grbovic, M., Lerman, K., & Mantrach, A. (2015). Evolution of Conversations in the Age of Email Overload. 603-613. *In Proceedings of the 24th International Conference on World Wide Web (WWW '15)*. https://doi.org/10.1145/2736277.2741130.

46   Hoffman, J. (2019). *The Ultimate Guide to Prospecting: How Many Touchpoints, When, and What Type*. HubSpot. Retrieved 2022, from https://blog.hubspot.com/sales/the-ultimate-guide-to-prospecting-how-many-touchpoints-when-and-what-type.

About the Author

Juliette Sander was born in France and grew up between Paris, London, and Brussels. After graduating from Wellesley College with a BA in Cognitive Science, she worked as a Research Assistant at the Massachusetts Institute of Technology. Having transitioned to sales, Juliette now lives in London and manages a high-performing sales team. Outside of work, she enjoys hiking and you can usually find her planning her next trip.